WELCOME

The

DARKNESS

By

Bachman Carpenter

A Dark Cyde Publication, New York

2

This book is dedicated to all the people who have brought unnecessary pain to my life. For without you, this book would have never been possible. You know who you are.

Time takes it all
Whether you want it to or not
Then all we see is darkness
Sometimes in that darkness we find someone
Only to lose them again in the darkness

-- Stephen King

Contents

6

8

The Shadow Of Brilliance

Despair is what fuels you

It puts the pen to the paper

Makes you reach the high notes

Bust through the finish line with a second to spare

Holding up the gold

Tears rolling down your face

Your father died the night before

You turned the hurt into fire

Making it impossible for you to lose

Sometimes you eventually find yourself

You can even crack a smile

This is no time to be productive

For all greatness you must suffer

I don't know why this is the only way

It is all you know it to be

You must be in the dark before you can see light

And without pain, there is no need, nor desire to create

Incapacitated

How do you figure?

I feel stuck inside a picture

That sits on top your TV

The reflection you see is not really me

Some guy smiling with a goatee

I agree that you think it's your one and only

Behind the smile it's dark and lonely

Sewn together melancholy

Not a phony bone in my body

I don't have much to offer you

But one plus one equals two

I guess that's better than being alone

In real life I'm just thrown together

Hair all messy

Worn out leather

But I'm givin' it my best, see

It's just easier in a dream

I'm walkin' a crooked beam

And a theme that I can't seem to change

A life that I can't arrange

A world to which I'm estranged

Can't even tell you my own name

Inside Looking Out

I'm looking at all your faces

Hearing all your prayers

Memories of times we shared

I didn't know how much you cared

The smell of flowers fill the room

I lay four feet off the ground

Crying and sniffling are the only sounds

Soon to be buried under a dirt mound

How the hell did I end up here?

Think of all the things I could've changed

But everything just stayed the same

Maybe I should've just changed my name

And there is this man in a funny suit

Saying so many nice things about me

And none of it's true, it just can't be

The bright white light I cannot see

I wonder what my family thinks

Will I see my dad, is this whole thing real?

The few more years I couldn't steal

It is the end, no more cards to deal

Calling One In

I dreamt you were wandering in the dark

In a big open field with no trees

Couldn't stay asleep as I tossed and turned

I tried to get back to the dream

When your life came to an end

I lost a piece of me

Could it really be?

That I'd never see you again

As my thoughts were undressed

All my words were suppressed

Like an uncovered book on the shelf

Trying to find my original self

But I need your help

What am I supposed to do dad?

Did you have it so bad?

You were supposed to show me how to be a man

Do you understand what this has done to me?

Christian and Claudine

Lost in a deep, dark sea

If I could just talk to you one more time

Maybe it would help me find

The cure for the things that infected me

Recapture my serenity

Ready to be set free

Sell Or Die

Look at you...

In your clean cut world

Thousand dollar suit

Italian leather shoes

Makin' that green

Steppin' on toes

Who fucks the most people?

Did you get the most votes?

Your diamond studded watch

Or your fancy sports car

Maybe a second home

Or the classic speedboat

Did you ever sit and think?

About the people that you hurt

Have you looked into the mirror?

Do you see the piece of dirt?

The devil's looking forward

To your early untimely death

He'll suck you through the pavement

Before you take your final breath

Shade Of Light

More often than not

This feeling comes over me

It's too difficult to explain

Like the living dead, but not quite the same

A blind man can see in his dreams

And as he wakes up screaming

He realizes he can see pain the same as us

Not willing to discuss the visions

Pinpoint to precision where everything went wrong

Not long for this world

Try to get back to sleep

Don't make a sound

It just might come back 'round again

The dreams we had when we were children

But it's all over...

And nothing will ever be the same

You can blame everything on the world we live in

Wipe off your stupid grin

This place is not fit for humans anymore

Even though we're the ones who destroyed it

What I would do to be a boy again

The Story I Love To Hate

It doesn't really matter

No reason to watch any further

The story always ends the same

Happily ever after is the name

If this was only true to life

I wouldn't carry around a knife

Hiding the scars on my face

And the ones in a deeper place

I'm not the prince that takes you away

I'm the devil on a dark cold day

My eyes can leave you feeling hollow

But they'll dare you to come and follow

Everything ends up good in the end

Is the message they try to send

What really happens is far, far worse

Your life is ruined, then your life is cursed

So the next time you shed a tear

About that movie with the lucky queer

In the real world it's a different thing

They'll slit his throat with a metal string

Man With A Plan

Life started out so simple

There was love all around

It wasn't long before I found out

That I could do anything

If I just put my mind to it

But it wasn't always a great fit

Because me and the rest were quite different

So I became a leatherneck

It was discipline that I needed

Traveled the world

Came back and found my wife

Had two boys and a girl

I gave them everything I could

But then there came a time

When I could give them no more

My life had become a chore

And I didn't know what was in store for me

By this time you had all gone

But I still had your pictures

On my forever lonely walls

My mind was no longer clear

In a vehicle that I could never steer

And I couldn't stop this fear of what's to come

I remember a time...

When there was still something left for me

But no one can see

Where this world is heading

Could it be that I'm the only one

Maybe it's time I bought that gun

And end this needless suffering once and for all

First Love

Maybe it's in the way

You unknowingly torture my soul

It just might be the reason

Why I still love you so much

It's strange how every single woman

Can never match up to you

And every single one

Is subconsciously being compared

When I see one that looks like you

I start to believe

I can find you in them

But you never seem to be there

I have grown tired of searching

And I am surely tainted

As long as this ache inside

Decides to stay around

I don't know why I am so sure

That you are my only salvation

Because I enjoy nothing

The way I enjoyed it with you

Then please tell me why

Even when a love story ends happy

I still feel so sad inside

It all just makes me want to cry

I'll love you until the day I die

Know It All

How can you be so blind?

Busy swingin' from your vine

Never able to find the things on the tip of your tongue

Or maybe you're just too young

Binding you to a life of ignorance

Putting up a tough stance

You're just a fool

Don't forget I'm smarter than you

And I'm more square than cool

But it's not fair to let people go on listening

To opinions with no relevance

Dancing around your delivery

Wishing they were home, asleep

Dreaming of times when you weren't there

Knowing deep inside that they just don't care

A pair of fists should do the trick

But you slipped out before it became a mess

The best thing you could've done

You're no fun at all

Hitting a wall five minutes in

As long as you're there we just can't win

Outcast

Once you've looked into the darkness

You carry it with you the rest of your life

There's no relief in sight

No walking through the meadow on a sunny day

Nothing but pain, and rain in your face

No place to hide

The feelings that won't subside and go on

Gone are the days of peace in my heart

No fresh start, no new beginnings

Fear keeps on winning

Bound to a life of solitude

Unless you're pussy or food or my workweek

There's a leak in my brain

Can't say I'm ashamed of it

I don't know why it's there

Don't have the capacity to care

Would I be better off dead?

The voices in my head won't stop talking

See me on the street, keep on walking

Don't turn around and stare at me

Because I won't share anything

It's where my world has come to

Aren't you glad you're you?

Famous Or Dead

Sitting in Hollywood today

In a rock star kind of way

Thank God I will not stay

In this place that's dark and vague

It's beaten me once before

When my feet couldn't touch the floor

It took my years of four

The closing of every door

Stockpiling the new fresh face

Won't you love me is the race

Sucking cock or whatever it takes

Can't go home and feel disgraced

Running tricks on the boulevard

Paying your bills are really hard

All this for that golden card

That says you won't be barred

From the famous and the hip

Or the clubs on the Sunset strip

Watch your step and do not slip

Or hell will have its grip

Then it will take its toll

Leave your body feeling cold

You slid right through the fold

Now you lose your soul

Let's Reminisce

You can't lose what you couldn't have

But you can lose what you could've had

Does it make you sad before you sleep?

No one sharing your sheets

Just the cat at the edge of your bed

It thinks it's getting fed, stupid

And it'll be dead in a short time

Then you'll go find another one

To remind you you're not alone

But you are, and you're getting old

Hair's gone gray and your souls been sold

Soon you wake from your slumber

Father Time's got your number

It makes me shudder to think

Didn't know you could sink this far

Leave the car running in the garage

Get barraged at the shrink

No time to think of what you're doing

Because you're missing that part of your brain

With no one to blame, where no one remains

Take a good look around...

It's the end of the game

Helpless

The ever spinning turmoil inside

The unsettling anxiety always there

Fleeting moments of solace

Almost like delusions of normalcy

You can see it in their eyes

They want to, but can't understand

They try to convince you they do

It's because they love you, and they're fresh out of ideas

You can't figure out why they're so happy

While you try to conform and fit in

You wonder if they can see right through you

The way you can see right through them

You sometimes sit and ponder

On what makes them so content

Everyday starts a new plan

Until darkness comes, and you give up again

Walking Blind

How do you make your friend your lover?

So they don't discover

How I cover my feelings

Am I not appealing enough?

All that wonderful stuff that I do for you

This is not brand new to me

I often wonder of what we could be

If only I could make you see

But it was not supposed to be

Because if it was, I wouldn't have to try so hard

And you wouldn't look so bored

And look so scared when my hand touches yours

You have me floored

I can't even think straight

Just dreaming of your face

Makes me forget my hate

Do you think I was just too late?

Could it be it wasn't our fate?

Well ain't that just great...

The 72nd Hour

It's a small window in a small world

Only a chosen few can go the distance

Through experience I've learned that I'm one of them

Obviously, this couldn't make me very proud

Being a soldier of a different kind

Somehow, it always seems I'm being put to the test

My competitive nature won't let me stop

I put on my gear, and head into battle

It's hard to explain the feeling you have

Watching the sun come up on the horizon

For the third day straight

Not having slept a wink

The fifth eight-ball clunks down on the table

You look at each other and smile

But boy do you know you're gonna pay for this

Everyday you're awake you'll hate yourself for two

Another one just dropped out

Ended up taking a cab home

That leaves just the three of us

One of you I barely even know

I hope the one I know doesn't want to leave

Of course, it doesn't really matter

'Cause I'm stayin' anyway!

Right until that last bit of powder disappears

Eventually, I make it out alive

Even though I've poisoned my body and soul

My heart continues to beat on

Maybe next time I won't be so lucky

Sometimes I'll see the guys from that night

I'll walk right by and hang my head

Like they didn't even exist

What used to be fun is now a nightmare

Evil Establishment

Things the government made

Like malt liquor and AIDS

Acid rain and crack cocaine

Get rid of the ones in pain

Cancer pills for pharmaceutical fame

Or give 'em a gun

Kill each other for fun

For some people, this world ain't ever gonna be right

Straight vodka and long white lines

Shitting out sunshine

You wouldn't know the dark if you went blind

It's all in your mind, although you'll never find it

They put the signs right in your front yard

And I know it's hard for you to understand them

So I'll give you a helping hand and tell you

Don't watch the news and read a book

Learn how to cook, avoid fast food

Get out of your car and take a walk

You'll be surprised at how far you get

And don't be a fool...

Happy endings are stories they haven't finished yet

Nice Knowing You

I know why you're leaving

Just like all the rest

I'm a little bit different

And it makes you feel out of place

There's nothing I can do

I won't change what I stand for

Nor would I want to

I just need someone that understands me

What makes a man a man?

Is it the choices he makes?

Or is it the way he follows through with them

Even if that means to make no choice at all

Someone once said to me

That I was a difficult man to love

So I looked in her face...and said

What the fuck does that mean?

But now I'm finding who I really am

And people are afraid of what they don't understand

Don't let the shaved head and tattoos fool you

Your patience will be your reward

Princess

It seems to me

That you're running out of chances

To be that person

You've always wanted to be

And it's not just me who sees

What's going on in your head

Maybe I should've said something sooner

You know, you're not dead yet

But you will be one day

And I'm sure you'll regret

All the things you didn't do or say

I guess you thought there was another way

To just breeze through life

Not caring what would happen

Back when you were a kid

You never got slapped

Or had to take responsibility for everything

I don't just blame you

I blame your parents too

For keeping your name out of anything

That could've got you into trouble

And it was all so subtle

But they had you fooled

And you fooled them too

Now you're getting old and you're alone

I can only hope that this has shown you

That you're not better than the rest of us

And if anything at all, it's even less than us

Holy Shit

Walking on the line of the void

No one knows what's over the edge

All the faith in the world can't save you now

Because you're gonna die, and we all die alone

Like the way you pray to God

Always feeling like you're being ignored

You feel betrayed, all the money that you gave

Pimping out the Lord, but where is he now?

I can't see Him, can you?

I can't hear Him either

Nor will you ever, but the delusions remain

You can only read about Him in a storybook

What a sick sense of humor He must have

Taking away all my family and friends

None of them knowing it was the end

You have a lot of fucking explaining to do

You want to give him ten percent of your salary

This mysterious man you've never met

I guess there's nothing I can do about that

But for me...there's no free lunches in this world

Revelation

As days and dreams fly by

We don't recognize the most significant times in our lives

And as the years go past

Defining moments never seem to last

Everything good ends too fast

And I would if I could

Change the way things are

Trade my time for a new type of journey

It begins in the mind and requires no money

If only I could find a piece of the puzzle

To alleviate the struggle

Before my mouth meets a muzzle

No time to play...busy working

To pay for things that don't matter to me

Loosely use the excuse that I'm free

Just a prisoner to society

Can't overcome the hurdles they've set in place

Can't finish first in the rat race

Is it too early to say?

Things are in a bad way

Family In Hiding

For a second

Draw your attention away from me

Now glance in the mirror

I hope it's what you're looking for

You can't hide behind me forever

Don't use me anymore

Your problems are your own

The chance to help yourself is fading

Does it make things easier on you

Using me as your scapegoat

It won't help you with your fears

They have nothing to do with me

I'm in a world all alone

This is what you chose

I had no say in the matter

Maybe it's all for the best

So stop being cowards

Change yourself, leave me alone

And always remember

I know who you are

Because I know who I am

But you don't know who you are

So you'll never know me

This is the way it has to be

Chance Meeting

My love was a novelty that wore off

Let me go get the sawed off

Because I can't let this happen again

And there's a message I need to send

I did everything you asked me to do

Then you had to go pull the Jew card

Well, I don't give a fuck what your parents want for you

What do YOU want, and what are YOU gonna do?

Your parents don't even talk to each other

And your father's balls belong to your mother

Do you really want us to be just like them?

Say yes now, you'll never see me again

Wouldn't even be able to be your friend

The end is near, here comes the fear

Not like a virgin ride on the Cyclone

Gonna die alone, heart breaks like a bone

I guess deep inside, it's how I want it to be

Walk around in my wears, dying slow as a tree

Lost ten pounds, available and free

Nothing serious for now... just let me be

Fistfuck

I didn't want a problem

But you started with me first

Now you're lying in the hospital

Calling for the nurse

If your friends weren't there to stop me

You'd be lying in a hearse

You could have left it all alone

But the choice you made was worse

I hate that you made me do it

The part of me that you steal

I keep trying to tell myself

That you people can't turn my wheels

Part of me really liked it

The way your jaw made my knuckles feel

Was it really worth it jackass?

Sucking a straw for your meals

I guess it's me that wears the dunce cap

As I'm sitting here in jail

I just talked to my lawyer

It's the last time I'll make bail

You'll never fool me again

I'll assure you I won't fail

I'm hanging up the gloves

Now watch this fucker sail

You, Me And The Universe

You should never believe

Just what you see

On the outside

There's always much more

It seems you were wrong

About everything

I can't teach you the world

You missed a few stops

Along the way

It's never too late

To learn just a bit

But it's gonna be hard

Because your mind is closed off

To keep yourself safe

From this horrible place

Overcome The Obstacles

It's not the roads you go down

But the ones you skip that have the answers

Answers to the questions you're afraid to ask

The task is at hand, take off your mask

For the first time take a chance

I promise it'll be over fast

But then you'll have had your first taste

Try not to waste it, it won't last

Now you've been bitten

And you need to get higher

Searching for blood like a vampire

Stick your hand in the fire, you won't get burned

It's fear that holds you back

But you've taken the first turn

Embrace the things you were told not to do

They're not smarter, just older than you

The things they told you were not true

They were just trying to keep you safe

And you bought it by the case

Now you want to rub it in their face

But they select their own memories

And will not remember

The things that they said

Enjoy watching them fester

Say no to the thought of parricide

You've just begun to live your life

Cut The Cord

You are not the saint you portray

I just don't look at it that way

No one ever sees the way you can treat me

Back in the day you made me believe

Things are different now

And I've figured you out

From here on in you won't win

Because I've surpassed what you know

And I'd be willing to show you

If you just gave me a chance

So put down your dirty weapons

As you walk into my world

They don't work on me anymore

And I can even the score if I wanted to

It's lucky for you

That it's something you didn't program into me

Hurting people for thinking freely

I cried myself to sleep many nights

Not one day without a fight

You just might be the reason for all my pain

And I will take your name in vain

As long as you're still willing to hurt me

Until you see that keeping quiet is a good thing

If you want to bring us closer together

If I want your advice, I'll ask for it

You'll be sitting a long time, my life is mine

Disconnect

If I sense the end coming

I begin to detach myself

I'll put the distance between us

I can hurt you now, or hurt you later

Could it be my fear of rejection?

Or my fear of acceptance

My fear of failure

Or maybe my fear of success

The years go by very quickly

The changes happen very slowly

How dare you try to break into my fortress!

You didn't even chip the paint

If you let yourself become a part of this

It will never let you go

But know that you have no choice

Everybody leaves

Drunk Jerk Off With A Big Mouth

Guilt and innocence is just a matter of timing

But I only see the dark side of everything

And no one knows how much restraint I have

To not put his nose bone through his brain

And it's a shame, because I really want to

But I don't feel like doing six months

And it's not a fun time with that Riker's crew

I haven't thrown a punch in eight years

Still lingering is this fear

That people will think I'm queer

If I don't stick up for myself

And it's not a question if I'll win

To me it's a cinch, it's in the bag

I've never lost a fight before

And I'm not gonna start today

But I must say that the truth is

A real man doesn't need to fight

And a real fighter never needs to start

Because strength is within your heart

But deep inside, I cannot lie

I wanted to tear that fucker apart

Opposite

Life is nothing but a cage

A cell that binds you

Goals that you will never reach

Maybe it's time you lowered the bar

I won't count you out just yet

You're not done fighting the good fight

There are many things you still have to do

So many places going unseen

Certain scenarios are unattainable

Even though your teachers told you different

You can really hurt yourself trying

But one pain can lessen the other

Anything is NOT possible

Try to live within your means

Sometimes you can surprise yourself

On how far you can't go

It won't help if you're rich

It can't help if you're poor

Even if you rob the liquor store

Chances are that you won't go far

America's Pastime

Hitting home runs and throwing strikes

That's what my childhood was like

The one time I wanted to be pushed harder

But I just got farther away

Instead of millions a year

I share my shame with fear

Watching the pro's like they were my friends

And I was better than them, but their game didn't end

Everything since I've eventually failed

My ship has set sail, too late to make bail

Play on the team, a seamless scheme

Now I let out a scream to my fading dream

You don't understand the talents I waste

I just wanted a taste, too late to make haste

Not the money, the girls, the house, or the fame

I just wanted to play the game

Didn't care if you knew my name

Can't help but shoulder the blame

For the terrible choices

Can't silence the voices

Don't stack up to what I once was

I just did what everyone does

DNA

You filled me with so many fears

Making sure I was vulnerable to everything

Breaking down all of his hard work

Creating me in his own image

Why didn't you just let my father raise me?

Couldn't you tell that he was my hero?

Didn't you see the turmoil you were causing?

It's why I get so mad when you continue meddling

Do you think you did a good job?

Taking away my masculinity

Filling me with shame

Which lead to my utter lack of functioning

Did it ever occur to you?

That you would take away my sense of self

Even after seeing me fall

Did you have to kick me on the ground?

Answer me this...

Where is my father now?

Where am I now?

And where am I going to be?

Just A Forty Hour Drive

Just wanted to be connected to you in some way

Expected it to happen some day

But our prior union was rejected

So I collected my thoughts

Corrected my way of thinking you might say

Fought my fears of intimacy

Insecurities always win easily

Everything is not as it appears

Maybe we were never meant to be

It's been a real long time

I guess we're both doin' fine

But don't you miss me just a little?

Why don't you meet me in the middle

And as the world continues to move on love

It seems to shove me to the side

Finally our game came to an end

Would you take me as your friend?

Lend me an ear once in a while

Keep a smile on my face

Race you to the fishin' hole

As for the future...you never know

Living The Lie

Hey man, I live in L.A.

I'm at one with the universe

The almighty power of the cosmos

It's like, the energy is working through me

Dude, doors are opening for me everywhere

I'm working hard and have what it takes

Do you know what I mean, man

Can you see it in my eyes, man

Can you feel it, man

Maybe you don't understand

I'm going to a party in the hills tonight

Doing enough drugs to kill a small child

Missing my imaginary audition tomorrow

Going to the Coffee Bean when I wake up at four p.m.

Charging the five dollars on my parents credit card

Standing around, hope I get noticed

Doing real well...mom and dad

I'm gonna be...a star

The Ravages Of Age

Saturday night, ten o'clock

All is quiet on the block

A feeling of loneliness comes over me

Home alone...watching TV

And it's nothing that I haven't seen

I feel like I'm missing something

Like I was eighteen again

About to get drunk with my friends

Or get laid, and send her on her way

Those days are done, I've closed the door

'Course, girls don't knock on my window anymore

My friends are livin' the married life

Army of kids, annoying wife

And the boys aren't allowed to hang with me

I guess my reputation proceeds me

I pull out the book, think of who I can call

But I'm setting myself up for a fall

Can't walk tall if I'm sitting down

Leap off the couch, dust off my crown

Used to own this town, but it's changed around

Hit the ground runnin' but I can't find nothin'

Take off my shoes, put on some tea

Tonight it just wasn't meant to be

Sacrilegious

I may not believe in God

But I believe in the human spirit

I believe in greater things than me

And whatever that may bring

Do you really think there's more?

This is all there is

You live and then you die

There's no castle in the sky

No kingdom in the heavens

No wings that make you fly

It's just an institution

That leaves pollution in your mind

And no matter how hard you try

It's something you'll never find

No last rites, no Jesus Christ

No Noah's Ark, no Adam and Eve

Just a trick up their sleeve, to make you believe

In a mystery man that you will never meet

And you must give it all, if you want to receive

The guarantee

To be eternally free

From the bad things we see

...as long as you never leave

Siblings Separated

I care a great deal about you

...in my own way

Because I don't show up on Easter Sunday

Doesn't mean I don't love you anymore

For awhile, I didn't close any doors

Nor did I think you were ready to walk through one

You've always looked at me like a loaded gun

Loads of fun, but could never really trust me

That's why I let things be

You must see by now...it's been twenty years

Do you think you can push aside your fears?

I don't think you can, but I won't cast blame

It's all the same guilt from your catholic game

It's a shame that it took you so long

After some time I considered you gone

But you've decided you want to re-connect

I just don't think we have anything left

Left to tend my own garden

My heart has hardened, I beg your pardon

Did you think I was gonna wait around forever?

I can read your thoughts...you're not that clever

You think our ties are severed

But they're not, they go on

Just not in the ways that you want

Would you trade it in for a little more?

Without a risk there's no reward

Even half way is way too far

So wherever you go...there you are

One Perfect Day On Main Street

I wanted to be somebody

Until I realized I was nobody without you

Like the greatest love story never told

The things that unfold as life moves by

So much time has passed

If only you knew how fast I would go back

To that beautiful sunny day in Northport

When nothing could come between us

I put my trust in your hands

People lining the streets

Pictures in boutiques

The ice cream store and the five and dime

Now we've run out of time

But the sun shined down on us that day

Ducked behind some building to play

I'll never forget as long as I live

To touch you again...what would I give?

Your Reality Or Mine

It's so hard to love...

This cookie cutting world we live in

I see the masses driving to work

Talking to themselves

Sitting in traffic

Suits and ties

Coffee cups and cigarettes

There was a day...

Fishing by the stream

Chopping your own firewood

Breathing fresh air

Do I dare?

Go against the norm

Build my cabin in the mountains

Say goodbye to it all

Humanity

No one seems to understand

How much life really hurts

Maybe I just come from a deeper place

Please make no mistake

That the look on my face

Is not always how I'm feeling

But more like seeing the things around me

Mean nothing to you

And there's something I'd like to do

Crush your head with a brick

Take my cigarette, and flick it

As I walk away

And I won't think of you again

Because I'm done with everyone and everything

That used to mean something to me

Because life always moves

When I don't want it too

And when I do

It seems to come to a screeching halt

I want you to kick my skull 'til it falls off

Maybe I'll stop thinking such horrible thoughts

Or maybe not, and I'll continue on

Try to put a song in my head

Get rid of what's dead to me

And that's everyone and everything

School Of Hard Knocks Alumni

I hit you so hard

My hands in a cast

Remember what I said

If you're not first, you're last

I can't digest all this pain

So I give it to someone else's name

The song remains the same

Just blame me, like everyone else

I may be selfish, but I'm not ashamed of myself

I keep looking up to check the clock

I'm colder than a witches cock

Fill a sock half way up with nickels

Next person I see is in a pickle

'Cause it's not gonna tickle when I bust their skull

Creep through your window...knife's not dull

Lull you to sleep with a six inch cut

...what you see is your guts

When you take your last breath

I'll fuck your wife like a slut

I shut the door, there's jewelry around

Check out the window for cops on the ground

Choke the bitch out so she won't make a sound

Found a ball of hundreds in the dresser drawer

My pockets are fat as I scale down the wall

Got to take it slow so I won't fall

When you're broke and hungry you take the call

Hide And Seek

I really hurt myself the other day

Reaching for that golden ring

I don't have faith in many things

Because things have showed me that I shouldn't have faith

No more do I enjoy the chase

No time to waste

Sometimes my life is deeply troubled

Uncomfortable while humble

Sometimes my candle's dimly lit

So I try to shuffle things up a bit

Not much to do but sit and think

Dirty dishes in my bathroom sink

Fix the kink in my suit of armor

Work harder than a Goddamn farmer

To eat up all those precious minutes

And give me less time to torture my mind

Short on wealth and short on breath

Dreaming of my own death

But I keep it locked in a drawer

What do you think it's there for?

Bro

You're the one that I call brother

A profound understanding that only we share

The bond that can't be broken

Until one of us leaves this earth

Both coming from the same blood

You could never tell by looking at us

Or even as we open our mouths to speak

Not unless you stood behind us while we walked

Three thousand miles come between us

It sometimes weighs heavy on my heart

Deep inside I still feel at peace

Because you'll always be there should I need you

Just slightly younger than I

I tried to teach you the best I could

I never counted on how much

YOU would end up inspiring ME

Whenever speaking of you, I swell with pride

Can't wait to tell them how you're doing

It's easy to see how much I respect you

But it's even more fun watching them figure out you're my hero

Charade

I look into your eyes

And I can see your disgust

But it's not real

And it's not for me

It is for yourself

Because you are someone's wife now

Living in your buttoned down married world

But you still want to fuck me

Do you see the smirk on my face?

It's because I know what you desire

You've had other men inside you before

But you gave all that up

And you're regretting it just a bit

The new life you've chosen

You may play the part everyday

But you still want to fuck me

The sky is blue

No...it's more of a grayish-white

I love this song

What a surprise...you changed the station

That outfit looks good on you

You ask me if that's my best pickup line

You can make believe you hate me all you want

But you still want to fuck me

You could never be friends with someone like me

Always reminding you of the life you gave up

Thinking of what a good fuck I must be

And that's too bad...I'm so much more than that

It's a shame you'll never have a chance to find out

You've already convinced yourself of who I am

But I will let you continue this ridiculous game

Because it's fun for me...and I wouldn't fuck you anyway

Armageddon

First things first

I wasn't like this at birth

The meek won't inherit the earth

Because things are gonna get worse

No chance of getting better

Look around to find some

I dare you to find just one

Now where'd I put that gun?

You think this is fun for me?

Knowing my children can't be free

My nephew's twelve years old

He can't even leave his street

Pray to God, get on your knees

It's not gonna change a thing

Will you tell Him that for me?

If you want change, you have to change yourself

It's not gonna change itself

And all your secrets that are well kept

Pile of rage and lack of depth

It's all just swept under the carpet

Are you scared yet?

Imaginary Friend

Your rough exterior doesn't fool me

It's obvious you have much to hide

I can tell by the way you speak

With an empty hole inside

You don't have to be afraid of me

Be calm, don't be alarmed

I have come here in peace

I'm no particular harm

I remember watching you cry

Thinking you wouldn't fit in

I knew right then and there

That we would become good friends

You know I can feel your pain

We have much to discuss

We have something in common

And it tears at us

We don't know what it is

This thing that we share

I don't think I can help you

But you need to know that I care

We are one of a kind

Because you know how I feel

Where are you when I need you?

I wish you were real

Two Out Of Three

If you were gone

There'd be no reason for me to go on

And I know you understand me

I heard you sing it in a song

A song you wrote for me and daddy

Even though he was an only child

He taught us to be brothers

Sayin' "listen to your mother"

And "love one another more than anything else"

I can still hear his voice echo in my head

He may be dead, but I know he's still there

And I know he still cares

Sayin' "play with your brother"

"You boys better play fair"

It's the heart of our old man we share

And I don't care how much time goes by

Never leave your side, there 'til I die

Can't look in your face without wanting to cry

You look just like dad as a younger man

Like a young Marine, not afraid to stand

I need to ask you if you'd have this dance

Lets enjoy it all, 'cause it's gonna go fast

Feeling At A Loss

Do you miss me?

Do you miss the fight?

If you ever wonder what my life is like

Watch the last five minutes of Sideways

This is just one of my average days

In which I may or may not

Take that long ride

To escape and hide

From all that is you and my tortured mind

Threw my pride on the floor

You're not even nice in my dreams anymore

And as I settle the score

None of them are the way you are

Or the way you were, I should say

Isn't there any other way we can co-exist

Is it weird that I miss you?

And want you dead at the same time

Was it hard for you?

Or was it easy to find that special someone

That makes you feel butterflies

You know, I hope he dies too

But I don't know why

I just know that it's true

You can see it in my bloodshot eyes

The time will come

When you will know how it feels to lose

Still Undefeated

We'll go to battle again

On different terms and separate lines

Grab a pen and write my rhyme

Combine my thoughts

Of the fights I've fought

The lessons I've taught

The answers I've sought

But nothing stays around long enough

I guess I'm not that tough after all

But I still stand tall

And I can't recall a time I haven't suffered

I really wish I was bluffing

But there's still a lot of stuff that needs confronting

When you relax and reflect

What are the things that you see?

I see a blunt object hitting me

Can't make it out...it's too dark

And it's hitting me out of the park

But my bite is worse than my bark

Wake up stark naked and sweating like a pig

I want to go back in, continue to dig

Wonder if it's just a sign

I'll get 'em next time

Creature Of Circumstance

If you want to play with the big boys

You better bring the big guns

Just know that it's not all fun

And guns aren't toys

I can't lend you my voice

It's being used right now

You'll figure it out somehow

I'll understand if you want to get out

I am not what I appear on the outside

My conscience won't allow me to thrive

But I must maintain my appearance to survive

To keep it comin' in live

I'm loud and clear

Neither here nor there

I hide my fear

'Cause I really do care

Like a shadow at night

I disappear from your sight

Finish the fight that you started

Leave you broken hearted

Cruel World

Seeing what no one can see

Feeling what no one can feel

Not listening to another living soul

Because they have no morality

And it's the path of principal that leads to character

It's what everyone has forgotten

People of the world have become inhuman

I want to take them down to the rivers edge

Hold them under water 'til they stop kicking

Satisfying me, but of course, making me one of them

Does it make me a terrible person?

Wanting so many people to die

I wonder what my loved ones would think

I wonder what God would think

Well, don't you worry...they're on my list too

My father taught me to be tough

My mother taught me to be scared

I taught myself everything else

Well...my mother won

So I hide in the dark

Goodbye Bitch

December 5th, 1997

Was the day we started dating

But now I just hate it

And the way that we say things to each other

You bring me no happiness

And it's safe to guess

That you've made quite a mess

Out of something that I thought could be great

But I was far too late

At the age of twenty-eight I started this

With a meaningful kiss

But now I just wish

That we never met

And I'm willing to bet

That I'm not the only one that regrets being with you

I wish I could just forget

The things that you did

To make a good man bad

You can look in my face

And say, how'd you get to this place?

But you helped turn me into what I was back then

How things have changed

Since someone reminded me

Of the way you treated me with lies and deceit

And at the very least

You could have let me go two years before

And not close the door on the rest of my life

Convincing me you'd be my wife

And that you'd love me to the end

All the rules we would bend

We would mend anything

Just another lie

I could never be friends with someone like you

Because now I'm grown

Fuck...I should've known

Obscurity

I would love to go home right now

Problem is, I don't have a home

It's in the eyes that it shows

The phone's never ringin'

Never hear me singin'

More like cursing while I whisper

Forming like a blister

Sinister is what you might think of me

How 'bout letting me be?

And letting it go

Then maybe time won't move so slow for you

Just looking for a place to rest my head

Maybe share my bed

And not wind up dead

I said it before and I'll say it again

Leave me the fuck alone

I just don't blend

Just a handful of friends

And they'll be none in the end

But being alone is not the same as being lonesome

Maybe I'll start a new trend

Don't Hurt Yourself

You take a good look at me

You try to describe what you see

But you look like you're struggling

It's because I'm not on the level

I'm half philosopher, half daredevil

Clothes disheveled or a three piece suit

Big Macs or fruit

And I'm not in the zone

But I'll break your bones

So you can't use the phone

And still...you won't leave me alone

Not a laugh or a sigh

More like crying

Like when King Kong dies

Or a bird that can't fly

The river's running dry for you

But you keep trying

What can I say, it's your dime

So you're gonna give it another run

But you can't lift my ton

Or move it to the side

Because I'm ten feet wide

Now you're running out of places to hide

But I was gonna leave you there anyway

I'm from the other side

You Had Your Chance

I wish you'd take me serious

But you treat me like a clown

If I'm on the top of your list

The list is upside down

No more time to frown

I took matters into my own hands

I wasn't about to stand around and wait

While I was filling myself with hate

It opened the gate to a whole new land

One where family doesn't exist

It's not what I wished, but the best I could do

Protecting myself from you

I think it's plain to see

That you didn't want me around

Stomping my heart on the ground

Feeling lost, and not to be found

Things haven't changed throughout the years

Like I don't have ears and I don't have eyes

Blaming me for your fears and lies

Maybe you just wish I'd die

Although you'd never say it

It's in the back of your mind

You haven't realized that I just don't care

And it's been this way for quite some time

I didn't want to be an outcast

If only you had asked, I would've shared in your fun

But there's no pictures of me in the family album

If the phone doesn't ring, it's me

You are where you want to be

Closure

The day has finally come

To set the old feelings free

Giving back a piece of me

The time we shared is done

I can't believe it took this long

To realize you were never there

You made me believe and that's not fair

But that's okay, 'cause now you're gone

Thanks for giving me that last long talk

Without it, I would still not know

If your feelings would ever show

The light that could make me walk

I will not forget the good times we had

For you, there's been many since us

For me, I've been afraid to trust

But that's over, and it's not so bad

Thanks for teaching me so many things

Best wishes I would like to send

This chapter is at an end

A bright future this will bring

Apparition

I saw a vision of you

Sitting in the chair across from me

You were the younger me

Unafraid...happy

Unable to see the pain that lies ahead

Soul alive, glimmer in your eye

Like looking into a mirror

Minus the fear, now things are clearer

Why did you appear?

Whisper in my ear

Is there something you'd like to say?

Why today, and not years ago

Just looking at you makes me want to cry

I want to pull you close

Tell you "don't be shy"

Spread your wings and fly

You can do anything you want

Move far away from this place

Miles away, maybe outer space

Now get out of here and don't look back

Keep that smile on your face

Roam

The drifter rides into the sunset

But where does he go?

And will he remember his travels

On the long healing road

He is a loner by choice

As he stares at the mountains

And rides through the plains

Soaking in everything he conquers

As for me, I'm just another cowboy

Trying to find my place in the world

My steed isn't quite the same

But my integrity still can't be sold...

And nothing ever feels like home

Fishtank

Ahhh...that's the life

Living in the twenty gallon world

Colors bright, red and blue

Wish I could be in there with you

But I can't, though

I must go

With the flow

Of this human life, so

Here's your food

Fill your world with shit

Until tomorrow

Here again I'll sit

Christmas Miracle

My beautiful little outlet

The only thing that's left

In my imperfect family history

The single sacred sacrament

We will be together on that day

My brother and my sister

My mother and thoughts of my father

Until the day I die

The journey of my heart

Has taken many turns

On the twenty-fifth of December

It is always in the same place

The opening of presents

The smell of a home cooked meal

The only day of the year

That I am truly at peace

Shenanigan

It's time you turned a new page

You try to hide it, but I can feel your rage

Stuck in a birdcage, only bigger

Going backstage like a gold digger

Snapping men like a twig

Snorting coke off a dick

You think you're real slick, but I can see through you

You may have them fooled, but I'm on you like glue

And I know how upset you get

That I know, that you know, that I know

Try to change the show, but I'm not buying it

Dress like a saint, but look like a misfit

So here's a little tidbit, you nitwit

You CAN'T shine a piece of shit

Accept who you are, it's okay to be bad

I could've been the best fuck you ever had

Make believe you don't care

But it's not me that's scared

We have something that will never mend

I'll hold the cup up in the end

Reflections

Mirror, mirror on the wall

Smash! Take that motherfucker

Seven years of...how do I look?

I didn't like what I saw in you this morning

There comes a time in everyone's life

When you see where you've come from

You see where you could have been

But you end up seeing where you are today

The mirror never lies

Neither does the lines on your face

Nor the bags under your eyes

Or the hour it took you to get out of bed

Do you think there's still time?

To hold the world in your hands

You know I'm your biggest fan

Mirror, mirror on the floor

Wanderlust

Stay too long in one spot

My blood gets hot

Never leaving home is a poor mans drug

Still a Long Island thug

And a little bit smug

Time to get back on the road

I follow a different code

Loosen the load, find myself again

Feel better than I've ever been

As soon as everything's in my rear view mirror

Things begin to get clear

But objects are closer than they appear

See some signs for South of the Border

Fillin' a tall order

Sit beside the saltwater

Somewhere in South Florida, 'til I can go no more

Start headin' west to the Cali' shores

Score some junk and find some whores

I'm not bored anymore

Hittin' it hardcore on the west coast

I think I like this place the most

So I get my fill and start to pack

Grab me a snack and start headin' back

Uninvited

If you could only see

How much this situation has affected me

You would have clearly tried harder

Harder to make me more a part of

Part of my immediate family

Instead you hung me from the family tree

Hung me out to dry

Didn't care if I cried

Didn't care if I died

And by die, I mean kill me a little inside

My insides began to rot and stink

While you were tickled pink

You never thought to think

On what this might be doing to me

What this might be doing to my life

Still have questions about my sharp knife?

The good news is...I'm stronger than you

Not just physically, but in my mind too

And I only have me to thank

Let me be frank about your lifelong prank

What you did to me is unthinkable

The way you disabled me

Making it impossible for me

To be part of a family

So if you wonder why I disappear early

Or if I don't show up at all

I don't want to be set up for a fall

You all really dropped the ball

Something Missing

Through good times and bad

Whether I'm happy or sad

There's a feeling I cannot bare

Something that's just not there

Wish I could tell you what it was

Or even what it does

Or how it makes me feel

Like life isn't even real

The feeling never goes away

It lingers every single day

Every moment I'm awake

Even my dreams it comes to take

It's brought me all over the world

To the beds of many girls

I talk to friends from far and near

But it's something I cannot hear

Nor can I touch or see

This thing that burdens me

It doesn't go away with a pill

This empty void I long to fill

If you know the secret, please let me know

So my life can begin to grow

Into something that matters to me

And to know how it feels to be free

The Sea Cleanses All

I stare at the ocean

And I wonder why

I can't have these things

Capable of such wonderful dreams

And even more horrible nightmares

Although it may seem

That I have my life in order

Nothing could be further from the truth

And I can show you the proof

When you look in my eyes

It's not the sky that you'll see

But a small piece of me

Dying slowly, but still alive

I'm not sure that I'll survive

But I'll still try anyway

It's not like this everyday

But just another phase and I'll tell you this

You've been blessed and not cursed

You wouldn't understand the worst

Because you're lucky my friend

But there's something that you don't have

It's the message I send

That I'll take to the end

Jesus And My Father

I can't hate them for who I am

They did the best they can

Now it's up to me

To let myself be

They gave me the tools

I guess I'm the fool

Can't provide for myself

Collecting dust on some shelf

I pump my fist at the sky

Pray for someone to die

But it's all in my head

It's my spirit that's dead

I look for someone to blame

But it's me that's ashamed

For what I've become

Wanting all, having none

I curse God and my dad

For the things I don't have

Where the fuck did you go?!

I wasn't ready for this show

If I see you someday

You better find out someway

To explain things to me

And set my soul free

Dingbat

You're a cunning little animal

But only when you have to be

It's amazing how you do it

Turning the knob on the naïve dial

You always know how to get what you want

Never looking evil while you do it

But you are, aren't you?

Well, you're not fooling me you fucking bitches

You know, there's a comedy to it

You don't know what the hell you want

Using your twisted powers to attain it

Trading it in, on the slightest whim

That's right, I'm talking about you

You stupid silly girls

The day will come where you meet me

When I'm finished, I'll show you the door

Don't let it hit you on the way out

Make sure you look real hurt

Don't worry, I won't tell them you were a slut

Because I just don't care at all

You'll find a new sucker tomorrow

A pussy ass yes machine

I'm sorry you couldn't get that from me

Oh, and thanks for the blowjob...cunt

Identity Crisis

Still looking for that white picket fence

Everyday I keep on searching

Going to the wrong places

Knocking on the door of an empty room

You can run away from your past

If you just try hard enough

You must prepare to re-visit it

Almost always at the wrong time

At least I still have my faith

Of course, my church differs from yours

Whether watching the waves crash

Or getting to the crest, to catch my breath

Still always asking the question

What am I doing here?

So many things testing me

But my character cannot be bargained for

I wonder if a time will come

When I will be forced to make a decision

To drop off the face of the earth

Or build my own white picket fence

Gray Skies In Fall

Since I turned twenty

I've only felt about ten percent of the time

Maybe it's a sign, the smoking gun

Left in my dreams of what's to come

Sometimes it's even fun

But it always ends up as nothing

As another day comes to a close

I don't even know

Where I'm supposed to be right now

And I can't even define the word normal

As I watch the leaves fall

And accumulate in the street

Say goodbye to the heat of summer

Smell the fresh chopped lumber

And the look of wonder that no longer comes to me

A hollow shell of what I used to be

Back when I was a kid my thoughts were free

But now I have to pay for it all

Can't even throw around the ball

Because my father's dead

And my brother's walking tall

Somewhere on the west coast

And my arm's not that strong

And this means it's not long

Before the snow starts to fall

That's when I hop in the truck and run

To someplace where the sun always shines

I'll make my escape under the light of the moon

And I won't come back 'til the flowers bloom

Then it starts all over again

Autumn will be here soon

Innocence Fleeting

That's my little girl

Up there on the stage

I have to choke back tears

As I listen to her play

Because when she plays

I'm amazed

At how nothing sounds the same

But the same feeling comes over me

Because it's the keys

That help me see

And reminds me

Of how beautiful life can be

And she's only thirteen

But right from the start

From the day she was born

She put a smile in my heart

Never to be apart

This person that I've created

Tried not to fill with hate

And make sacred the things that really matter in life

Until the knife comes down

In the form of a boy

Who wants to make her his wife

That's my little girl

Out there in the world

Destiny Alone

They say that being in love

Is how you know you're alive

Maybe I'm dead

Or could this be a dream

Sometimes I want to scream

But I'll keep it inside

Instead of letting it all out

Why be healthy now?

On this one I'll take a bow

To the powers that be

They're stronger than me

They've beaten me, you see

Maybe I'll catch them some time

But...I probably won't

I lie here in silence

Constructing my fence

Five Stages

You've never really lived

So you die a bit inside

Cry yourself to sleep

Sleep inside a box

Box it all up tight

And you never really die

Live inside a lie

Lie beside a stranger

Strange as it may sound

Not yet underground

A smile that's never real

Real to everyone but you

You touch, but cannot feel

Feel it's time to disappear

Overcome by all your fear

Maybe it's all been a dream

A dream of being free

Free from what you've seen

You've seen too much already

Never kept it straight and steady

I think you're in denial

And this makes you very angry

So you decide you want to bargain

And you fall into depression

You just have to accept it

Sensitivity Training

I can resist

Anything but this

And this is that

As I crack my wrist

I must use my fist

To fatten your lip

I just can't help it

Say goodbye to your lisp

This brings me no bliss

And it's not a short list

It might make you sick

Stick around, I insist

You just don't see it

We're not a good fit

My knee is the ball

And your face is the mitt

I just wanted to sit

Relax, drink a bit

You couldn't let it go

So I punched out your shit

Your nose is all split

There's blood in your spit

Please leave me alone

You all make me sick

Pipedream

Life is nothing but a series

Of hopes and disappointments

I have begun to become weary

I prefer to have no one near me

Unless someone could please hear me

Then I wouldn't feel that I'm all alone

It seems that I've already stopped existing

Like an inmate on death row

Just a pile of burned bones

Say a prayer for my damned soul

They say it's the most brilliant

Who have the most persuasive demons

Is that why I'm on a strong slant?

It's probably why I still can't

Feel like anything but a small ant

You know you can't break me

Because I'm already broke

Does it appear to you that I'm crazy?

It has nothing to do with being lazy

And it doesn't matter what anyone says to me

You must be willing to risk everything

In every moment of time

Or you have certainly gained nothing

When everything sounds like the wrong thing

Hasn't my life been worth something?

Deli Girl

I believe I've met my equal

In that girl behind the counter

Can I have my sandwich now?

And an extra large side of sarcasm

Don't forget to look me in the eyes

When you're giving me my change

Would it sound silly if I told you?

That it made me feel funny inside

You know, I don't even drink coffee

It's just an excuse to see you

I pour it out when I leave the lot

Or give it to the homeless guy on the corner

Today, I'll have the oat bran muffin

Can you put some wise-ass remarks on that?

You make sure I leave with a smile

Thanks for making me feel special

You put my number in your pocket

You could have just thrown it away

Instead I try to figure out

What you're thinking, every morning

The day had come where I realized

Nick the salesman and Bobby the plumber

We were all one in the same

It's a shame, I didn't get to know you

I think it's about that time

I find myself a new deli

I know they won't make me feel like you do

But at least I'll save a buck on coffee

Rough Neck

Covered in ink, but silky smooth

Ain't no fag and I ain't no fool

East coast attitude meets west coast cool

Pay attention, while I take you to school

Not afraid of bangers

Not afraid of slummin'

I'm like the wind

You never saw me comin'

You know I just walk straight through the jungle

Won't avoid the lions, or avoid the struggle

Don't be concerned with the junk I smuggle

There's only one man in my tight knit huddle

Play the game

Knuckle sandwich in your lunch bag

Missed your name

I'll read it off your toe tag

Didn't see the hook that blackened your eye

Now you're flat on your back, starin' up at the sky

You never had a chance, I'm like the samurai

I'm more afraid to live than I am to die

What don't you understand?

What is it you can't see?

I'm not above you

But you are beneath me

Gun in the belt, knife in the sock

Always move alone, never with the flock

You better run and hide when you hear me knock

'Cause I'm the baddest motherfucker on the block

Imagine That

I'll find the bastard that did this

He's taken my freedom

Made it hard to see the things in front of me

At this point in time, you couldn't stop me if you tried

If only I knew who to blame it on

My troubles would be gone

But I can't blame it on me, you see

Because that would mean everything's my fault

No reason to throw salt in my wounds

Stare at the moon, start the prowl

Growl like a wolf as I hunt my prey

But it's nowhere to be found

And still I remain angry...how profound

I've covered a lot of ground these past years

But my fears have not subsided

Which leaves my hope divided

Into two things that don't matter to you at all

So I fall, but I get back up

Have a cup of beer at the bar

And there's this guy on the far side staring at me

Maybe he knows me

Or maybe not, and he wants to go

Time for me to put on a show

The people gather 'round and start screaming

The familiar sounds of bones crunching

That's my cue to leave

Head home, wonder if it's finally done

But it's all in my imagination

Message To A Dead Man

I can't believe it's been eleven years

Since I've talked to you

I miss those days

When you would come into my room

You'd tell me that everything would be okay

You don't have to worry

I know how much you loved me

You showed me all the time

I miss your hand on my shoulder

And always saying yes when I said no

I remember seeing you get choked up

When I pitched that no-hitter

I could tell you were proud

Those were some good times

I wish we could have some more

I understand now why you had to go

I wasn't ready for you to leave me

I know you had your reasons

If I had just one more night

We'd play darts at the bar on Evelyn Drive

So many more things to tell you

But I guess it's about that time

I sure hope that we meet again someday

I know I'll have to die to get there

But it's something to look forward to

Our Secret Dinner

With both of our heads on the same pillow

Time seems to slow down to a speed I don't recognize

And as I look in your eyes

I can see things about myself that I didn't know existed

Although I always wished that they did

There's a light that surrounds you

The aura around you is not parallel to mine

It makes me want to be on the same line

Makes me feel I can find myself again

Like I was ten years old

With no worries in the world

I want to curl up with you and die that way

And I have to say

That I never thought I would feel that way again

But I was wrong

You make me want to write a song

If only I could sing it to you

I could show you how much you mean to me

And how you help me see

That everything isn't so bad after all

That the important things can't be bought and paid for

Helping me keep my feet on the floor

Making me clearly see the signs

I'll wait for you 'til the end of time

The Finish Line

Thirty-six years old

And not much to show for it

Too afraid of being hurt

It's why I'm always alone

Just cut me, and get on with it

Don't give a shit, just spit on me

Whether in my dreams or reality

I think it's plain to see

I carry on no legacy

My last name dies with me

Unless my brother feels differently

Although we see eye to eye on many things

There's no one pulling his strings

Is my life tragic?

Or should I be ashamed

Just remember my name

When I go down in flames

Not for the things I've done

But for the small way I've won

No more will I have to hide

When I beat you to the other side

Outlines Are Clear

Don't want to get out of bed

Don't want the day to start

But my mind is connected to my heart

And it tells me to get up and get going

My age has begun showing

My body has begun slowing

Not ready to throw in the towel just yet

And I'll bet you can't guess

That I'll accept nothing less

Than the best I can be

I've had my share of troubles

As I rummage through the rubble

And I'm fearless in a way that you will never know

Locked inside your bubble, and not allowed to go

The places I've been, the feelings I've felt

The cards I've been dealt

Might tell you there's not much left of me

You think you know, don't be silly

There's more to Billy than meets the eye

I'll be standing over you when you die

The Devil

Sweet smelling tobacco

The prick of the needle

The bullet holds two grams

There's a little left of the sour mash

Big bankroll

Football field yacht

The luxury sedan

The occasional swim in your mansion

The doctor that saved your life

The lawyer that kept you out of prison

The friend that banged your wife

Even your accountant screwed the system

But most of all it's them

With their round tits and firm asses

Long hair to hide their horns

Evil comes in many forms

Effexor With No Effect

Happiness makes even the meekest boast

My elusive ghost, an imaginary host

It's hatred that focuses the mind

The dark side...things of that kind

Helps you find out who you are

What are you looking for?

Tired of being bored

Wish you were never born

They give me these pills that will make me "better"

Maybe now I'll be sure

But my brain wears a sweater

I don't think they're working

Demons are still lurking

And with no one to live up to

I prefer to be awake, thank you

With the remainder in the garbage

My perception is transcendent

Although my sadness is informal

I start to return to normal

With no money and another's wife

Just change in my pocket and a sharp knife

Check under the seat for the lead pipe

Back to a day in the life...

21

I see all your beautiful faces

Reminding me I'm not getting any younger

If I could just go back a few years

I'd be taking you home with me

I see the young men standing around you

These are the guys that have taken my place

And if I do say so myself

I was better than them

Even though I'm borderline to you

You still have some respect for the old player

You know you can have me if you want

Just remember, it used to be the other way around

It just hit midnight

And my eyes are getting tired

There was a time way back when

I would just be leaving the house

Decline Of Civilization

Contrary to what people say

I believe intelligence is a curse

And to make matters worse

They think I'm a born loser

My I.Q. would just confuse them

I blame society for the simple

The stupid as a pimple

Can't even fill a thimble

With what they think they know

No space left to grow

Until I throw them a curve

Watch them duck and swerve

Hoping to hit a nerve

As I'm connecting with a left

I'm committing brain theft

I have no one left to talk to

Because I'm always five steps ahead

Are you an imbecile or dead?

Walking zombies that are well fed

Idiot convention in the lobby

I need a new hobby

To All The Girls I've...Loved?

My heart is swollen

My spirit's been stolen and taken for a ride

Crouch in the corner and hide

The feelings inside are polluted

Because peoples views are so deluded on what love is

Because you didn't tell me, doesn't mean you didn't lie

Omissions are betrayal

You can stick that needle in your eye now

It's okay...I'll wait...I have time...

I can't believe the things you did to me

But out of suffering came creativity

Brought me places I've never dreamed of

Helped show me the meaning of true love

And that what we had wasn't it

And that my world took a shit because of you

Now my hearts on the bottom shelf by itself

And I can't help but think it'll be there awhile

Filed your name off the side with the others

The only name left is my long lost brother

I'll be pissed for sometime with no release

For without anger

You can't understand peace

And at the very least

I suggest you look inside yourself

Get out the things that are wrong

Because it won't be long, before they're too far gone

Just don't come looking to me for forgiveness

All you'll get from me is "Fuck You Bitch"

Remember To Forget

The first time I saw the sun come up with you

I forced my eyes to stay open

I remember if I fell asleep

I'd never feel that way again

I'll love you forever

And never love you at all

You'll always be mine

Always and never

I wish I could let another through

If only they could break my barrier

Many have tried, and they've all failed

It might be nice to actually feel again

I hear it said everyday

Stop living in the past

What if your days are numbered?

And the best years are behind you

We all have places to which we must return

And by going back, we might finally leave

Almost like smelling the pillow next to you

Knowing already her scent has been washed away

I Miss You

Went to your funeral this morning

Did the eulogy

No one was there to hear it

What does that say about me?

In your name, I do a shot of the good stuff

I'll be with you soon enough

It's a long time to wait for one moment

Unless my loneliness is left unbroken

Truer words were never spoken

Than the ones I said for you today

No need to get on my knees and pray

I wish you could've stayed, but I guess it was your time

Now I'm alone on the front line

They never could define you

And I got the last interview

When they nailed the lid on the coffin

I hid in my skin

Tears rolled off my chin

I felt you by my side again

I promise I'll visit you soon

We'll have a drink under the moon

All good things come to an end

Until we meet again, my friend

Student – Teacher Night

You approached me because you think I'm unstable

You work your way in, and try to enable me

I'll sweep you under the table, and your desolate lines

If you want to break your bread that's fine

Just don't compare your life to mine

Put away the wine, you won't get in my head

Let me show you my bed...now it's time you left

And you seem quite adept, so I expect you to go

Because of the game that you throw

Did you enjoy the show?

You can teach an old dog new tricks

And you're pretty slick, but I invented this shit

I didn't ask you to sit, get the fuck out bitch

You've just been added to a very long list

The cuff marks on your wrists will be gone by morning

Please don't say I didn't give you fair warning

Never been accused of being boring

And it was all so alluring, but now you know what I am

Silent as a lamb, pulled you into my scam

Wham, bam, thank you ma'am

You say "Goddamn, I should've known better"

That's right...you should...put it all in a letter

Don't send it to me, send it to someone who cares

Perhaps you could've stayed, if you wanted to share

191 MPH

I live more in five minutes

Than most people live in their life

Danger is my spice

Not quite as nice, but more brave than you

My blood runs true

The rear tire tears the ground

Feels like the world turns 'round as I'm standing still

There's no pill that will bring me down

Front tire stands up and I stare at the sky

The good chance I'll die is a blistering high

That's the risk I'm willing to take

The pavement I break

The cops that I shake

The dreams that I make

There's no way to fake my exclusive creed

I'm a different breed, not afraid to bleed

Just a small offering to the God of speed

So you better take heed when you follow me down

Your heart starts to pound

You're surprised that you found

That you're no longer bound

The only sounds are that and the wind

To not know is a sin

And you'd much rather win

But to know what I know

You must first begin

Thanks For Nothing

The four of you shall remain nameless

Or as I refer to you...bad memories

I try not to speak of you by name

I don't quite think you're worthy of it

Each one of you having a part in my destruction

Spanning across twenty inadequate years

All of you senselessly crippling me

Making it impossible for me to "love"

I've tried to say goodbye to you so many times

But you always find a way to resurface

Whether it be that special song

That really good movie

Or the long walk through the woods

I know that you all have your own lives now

But I also know that if you're not alone

The man you're with is being tortured

I know this for sure, if I know anything at all

Just as sure as I know you're saying the same thing

I hope you're all doing real well

Of course, that's not completely true

I never could lie to any of you

Part of me wants the best for you all

Part of me wants to know what went wrong

Most of me wished you were buried in my yard

Nitroglycerin

My minute hand moves counterclockwise

Still don't have time, to find the right disguise

I realize I have nothing to get ready for

Throw my keys on the floor

Punch my fist through a door

"Why can't there be more" you can hear me whisper

Go buy some liquor

They say that it's quicker

My life starts to flicker in and out of a dream

Wake up with a scream

Drowned it out with Jim Beam

My self-esteem is taking a dive

Jump in the car and drive

As I arrive, I start feelin' alive

So my nose collides with a mirror

And I volunteer...first time in a year

That's when everything good just disappears

I feel like a deer in the headlights

Night turns to day and back to night

"But I'm reaching new heights"

So I write it all down in my book of pain

To describe and explain

On how I can't abstain

Or maybe just complain

As it starts to rain, I try to get some rest

Put my hand on my chest

Swear to do my best

Predator

To all the women I've hurt

Please accept my apologies

It wasn't my intention to cause you pain

Our feelings just weren't the same

I loved you all in my own way

Left you feeling you were part of a game

I just don't have the capacity to love

I thought that the right one would give me a shove

And I didn't think I was above any of you

Adria, Danielle, Tara and Sue

...Just to name a few

You were the glue that kept us together

Kept me light as a feather

But I change like the weather

And whether or not I decided to stay

You'd make me pay if I didn't play

Letting me know you were crying all day

I hid from your calls and stayed out of sight

Letting me know you were crying all night

I was just trying to avoid a fight

Please understand that I know I was wrong

And how bad I feel about what I've done

After all this time there's not much I can say

Just try to forgive me, somehow, someway

Two Halves

Maybe it's just doing your part

Or being a part of something bigger

All I can ever do is be me

Part loser, part winner

But a strong finisher

I think it's worth the gamble

You must avoid the scandal

If they get you in a corner

Hit 'em with a mop handle

Crack a beer, let go of the static

Lounge in the hammock, light up a smoke

Part rich, part broke

But my life's not a joke to me

Content with its diversity

Known to hide my creativity

So save your pity for someone else

For the feelings you've never felt

Don't have time for the likes of you

Too many things I have to do

Part false, part true

But my crew knows who I am

And nobody loves you at all

Because you have nothing to offer them

Bamboozled

I am the great illusionist

You will believe only what I want you to believe

A trick up my sleeve

The tangled web that I weave

But it got you to leave, so I know that it worked

It's one of the perks

So you think I'm a jerk

I just figure it doesn't matter that much

So you feel like a slut

While I strut my stuff

What did you think it was all about?

I fucked you on the couch

The first time we hung out

Please don't shout...and stop calling me

Consider yourself free, now just let me be

I'm on to thinner and better things

I've had three more flings just this week

Can't stand to be meek, it's perfection I seek

Didn't you have fun making my bedsprings squeak?

Now, I can't pull a rabbit from a hat

And my 'wand into flowers' trick just falls flat

I can't pull a quarter from behind your ear

But I'll have no fear, when I make you disappear

I know it sounds severe, but it's not that bad

And I'm sure that you know...you've just been had

Bugs

You're the only woman for me

The only one that's returned my love

Most perfect creature I've ever known

Gray and white, twelve pounds, seven years old

You know when I'm happy

And know when I'm sad

You know when I need some love

And when I need to be left alone

Wish I could take you out to dinner

Be the best date I ever had

Eat fast, no arguing

Back home to bed

Used to be clouds-changed it to bugs

After I found out your fascination

Your eight-legged friend eating disorder

I wish you could live another fifty years

I'll Drive

As I sit in the backseat of the car

I drowned out the sound of voices

Not far to go

Sad song plays low on the radio

Never knew the right time to cry

I'd rather die than show my painful side

Just wait a minute and hope it'll pass

Sometimes it goes rather fast

Not much in the tank today

I guess it's just another way

That God makes me pay

I wish it was May, but it's the gray of November

And I can't remember a time when I wasn't scared

I stare blankly with a glare in my eye

Thinking of how life's not fair

And I wouldn't dare ruin this silent moment

Not with a prayer, anyway...I know HE doesn't care

You can't tell by the way I wear my clothes

On the outside it doesn't always show

The things that go on under my skin

Loss of appetite keeping me thin

Life's a game of cards, you know I'm all in

Who cares if I win...rather be happy instead

Now I've made my bed, bad dreams in my head

And I dread every day that I'm not dead

Alter Ego

Boy, am I tired of hiding

And all the rules I must abide by

My money can't buy me pride

Can't decide if it's time to heal

Anticipation I can't feel

A freedom I can't steal

Is my conscience real, do I even exist?

I raise my fist

At this unexpected twist

A misty haze, confused and dazed

Undoubtedly brazen, won't see me prayin'

Feelin' blasé, but I'm still stayin'

Because things couldn't possibly get worse

And this may sound well rehearsed

But it's still my burden

An unavoidable curse

And no matter how hard I try

I can't reverse this living lie

Look up at the sky, let out a sigh

...wonder when I'm gonna die

My Turn

If you have a God given talent

You have to give a voice to it

Refuse to understand the word "quit"

Can't sit around when you scream it out loud

Entertain the crowd, try to reach the clouds

When my dad looks down on me I hope that he's proud

He never got a chance to see me start

But you can't break a broken heart

And my heart has turned into a stone

When I walk this life, I walk alone

Beside brain dead clones and orange cones

If only I'd known I could change the course

Find the source and then hit it full force

Divorce this life and start over new

When I get to the top and come into your view

Better get on your knees and shine my damn shoes

Kiss my ass or you'll be singin' the blues

Lose your stepping as I keep you guessing

Pray for a blessing as you change your dressings

You're welcome for the free lesson

Bachman would like to thank the following:

Christian Carpenter, whose tireless writing is what made me begin this whole thing in the first place, and against all better judgment, has decided to believe in me no matter what. Keith Kassan (Unc), for blessing me with the knowledge of all your worldly wisdom. Adam Wolf, for always listening to countless hours of hair-brained schemes. Jonathan Wolf, for always putting me in a better light. Gary Wolf, for never being afraid to come into the darkness with me. The extended Wolf family, for always making me feel I have more brothers wherever I go. Bryan Alec Floyd, whose writings made poetry my first choice. Last, but certainly not least, Gina Stacknick. Not just for all the help with the book, but for making me feel I can do anything. You're the only person that's ever completely understood me and decided to stay anyway.

About the Author

This self-proclaimed "jack of all trades" has disliked numerous employment opportunities such as...a car detailer, bartender, pool guy, model, mortgage broker, bouncer, and carpenter...just to name a few. He has also owned his own businesses including floor cleaning and restoration, vending machines, and landscape design and maintenance. He tells us the only thing he's ever really enjoyed is writing. That, and his small list of hobbies which include fishing, camping, hiking, reading, riding motorcycles and off-road ATV's. He has been riding motorcycles for twenty-five years and is a member of the American Motorcycle Association. This avid fisherman also belongs to the New York Sportfishing Federation.

To contact Bachman Carpenter for readings or signings, go to: nunsonheroin@optonline.net

www.ingramcontent.com/pod-product-compliance
Lightning Source LLC
Chambersburg PA
CBHW031254090426
42742CB00007B/450